I CAN PAINT

Author: Fiona Campbell

Edited by Matthew Parselle

Designed by Victoria Illiffe

Illustrated by Michael Evans
Photography by Steve Shott
Series editor: Paula Borton
Series designer: Robert Walster

© 1996 Franklin Watts

Franklin Watts
96 Leonard Street
London EC2A 4RH

Franklin Watts Australia
14 Mars Road
Lane Cove
NSW 2066

ISBN: 0 7496 2390 X
Dewey Decimal Classification: 751

A CIP catalogue record for
this book is available from
the British Library.

Printed in Malaysia

10 9 8 7 6 5 4 3 2 1

Before you begin

Make sure that you have all the things you need. Cover the surface you are working on with lots of old newspaper.

Things you may need:

ready-mix paint

stick glue

PVA glue

sponge

small decorator's brush

thick brushes

thin brushes

pencil

poster putty

poster paint

sticky tape

round-ended scissors

glitter glue

paper

Be prepared

Half-fill a jar with water. You'll need to fill it with clean water lots of times while you are painting.

Wash your brush in the jar lots of times as you paint. Try to keep your hands clean too.

Keep your paints in pots with lids or cover them with foodwrap and put them in a box with a lid.

Mixing colours

You can mix two different colours to make another colour.

red + green = brown

blue + yellow = green

green + yellow = bright green

yellow + red = orange

black + white = grey

3

Spoon creature

You will need:

bright paper

old wooden spoon

paints

masking or sticky tape

PVA glue

Add a red tongue to make a snake.

1.

Stick pieces of tape around the spoon. Leave some gaps.

2.

Paint all over the spoon. Leave it to dry. Peel off all the tape.

Glue the wings to the spoon to make a dragonfly.

3.

Paint on big eyes and lots of patterns on the stripes.

4.

Draw wings on folded paper. Cut through on both sides.

5

Rollercoaster

You will need:

long piece of paper

small potato, cut in half

small blocks of sponge

paints

1.

Draw a wavy line on your paper with a pencil. Then paint over it.

2.

Dip a sponge into some bright paint and print lots of shapes along the line.

3.

Dip one half of the potato in paint and print lots of heads. Add faces to them.

4.

Dip the other half of the potato in some paint and print lots of wheels.

5.

Paint lots of long, thin lines on your rollercoaster and leave it to dry.

Spotty dotty turtle

You will need:

scraps of coloured paper

sponge

stick glue

2 pieces of white paper

bubblewrap

bright paints or inks

1.

Use a wet sponge to make the paper damp all over. Add lots of splodges of paint or ink.

2.

Lay the bubblewrap on top. Carefully rub your hand over it then lift off the bubblewrap.

3.

Lay the bubblewrap, paint-side down, on a new piece of paper. Rub over it then lift it off.

8

4.

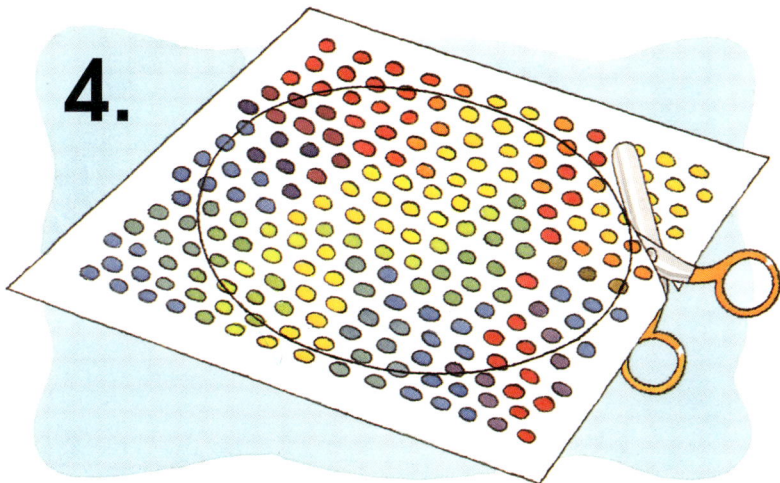

Leave it to dry. Draw a big oval shape for the turtle's shell. Then cut it out carefully.

Try using plastic foodwrap instead of bubblewrap.

5.

Cut out a head, flippers and the tail from the scraps of paper. Glue them onto the back of the shell.

Add some eyes.

Spider's web

You will need:

large piece
of paper

old plate (for
mixing paint)

paints

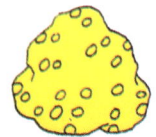

small chunk
of sponge

Glue on some
thread and
hang another
spider from
the web.

1. Mix some thin paint and sponge it onto the paper. Leave it to dry.

2. Paint a dot somewhere near the middle of your paper.

3. Paint some lines out to the edge of your paper with a thin brush.

4. Starting near the middle, add curved lines to make a web.

5. Carry on adding more lines as shown. Leave it to dry.

6. Paint a big spider somewhere on your web. Add some eyes.

11

Into space

You will need:

poster putty

paints

black paper

old toothbrush

scrap paper

1.

Draw some stars and one or two circles for planets on scrap paper. Cut them out.

2.

Draw half a rocket on folded paper. Cut through both sides.

3.

Stick all the shapes to the black paper with poster putty.

4.

Dip the toothbrush in paint. Drag your finger over the brush towards you to splatter the paper.

5.

Splatter on more colours. Leave it to dry then pull off the pieces. Paint the shapes using a thin brush.

13

Bowl of flowers

You will need:

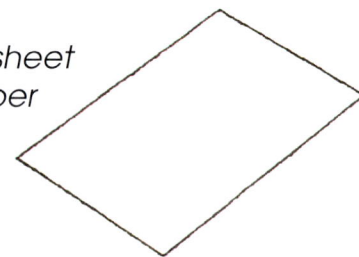

large sheet
of paper

paper plate

PVA glue

bright
paints

different round
things (mugs,
cups, yoghurt
pots)

*You could add
spots and stripes
to the flowers.*

14

1. Fold the paper plate in half and open it out again. Use scissors to cut it carefully along the fold.

2. Paint a bright pattern on one half of the plate. Glue it near the bottom of your paper.

3. For the middles of the flowers, draw around the round things. Leave lots of space between.

4. Paint the middles and add petals around them. Add stems and leaves in the spaces.

15

Monster meal

You will need:

*large piece
of paper*

knife, fork and spoon

paper plate

paints

1.

Put the knife, fork and spoon on the paper as shown. Draw round them.

2.

Draw lines across and down your paper for a tablecloth.

3.

Paint the knife, fork and spoon and the squares on the tablecloth.

4.

Paint a pattern around the edge of the paper plate. Add a huge, tasty meal.

5.

Add faces to the food to make each thing look like a scary monster.

You can glue the plate to the tablecloth if you like.

Snake in a basket

You will need:

PVA glue

large piece
of paper

flour

small piece of
paper (about the
size of this book)

small strip
of card

paints

tablespoon

old teaspoon

water

1. Use scissors to cut some V shapes in one end of the small strip of card.

2. Mix a tablespoon of flour with a little water. Add a teaspoon of glue and mix in some paint.

3. Use a big brush to paint the small piece of paper with the mixture. Do this very quickly.

4. Drag the cut end of the card across the paint to make patterns. Leave to dry.

5. Place this book at the bottom of the big paper. Draw a snake above it. Then paint the snake.

6. Fold the small paper. Draw half a vase and cut through on both sides. Glue it down.

Spooky sunset

You will need:

large piece
of paper

thin card

paints

small piece of
sponge

drinking
straw

1.

Mix some yellowy-orange paint. Dip the sponge in it and rub it across the large paper. Let it dry.

2.

Fold the card. Draw half a bat along the fold. Cut it out through both sides.

3.

Open out the bat and lay it on the painted paper. Draw around it.

4.

Draw another bat shape on the paper. Then paint both bats black. Add scary eyes and teeth.

5.

Mix some very watery black paint. Drip blobs of it at the bottom of your picture.

6.

Put one end of the straw on the blobs and blow hard to make the spooky trees.

You could make the second bat smaller.

Flash cat

You will need:

black paper

bright or fluorescent
paints

cottonwool buds

1.

Draw a circle for the head and
an oval for the body of the cat.

2.

Add some ears, legs and a tail.
Paint the outline of the cat.

3.

Paint some eyes, a nose and
some stripes on its body.

4.

Paint between some of the stripes and add lots of circles.

5.

Dip cotton buds into some paint and use them to print lots of dots.

Try painting other animals and decorating them with different patterns.

Flashy fish

You will need:

stick glue

white candle or wax crayon

old saucer

bright inks or paints

blue paint

paper towels

white paper

1.

Dampen two paper towels. Drip watery paint or ink onto them. Leave them to dry.

2.

While the towels are drying, draw wavy lines across your paper with the candle.

3.

Mix blue paint with lots of water. Wipe it across your paper with a paper towel.

4.

Cut out lots of fish from the painted paper towels. Glue them to the blue piece of paper.

24

Draw some green
seaweed with a
wax crayon.

Add some eyes
to your fish.

Hanging cones

You will need:

coloured paper

paints

large plate

thick thread or wool

glitter glue

sticky tape

1.

Draw around the plate on paper. Cut it out carefully.

2.

Fold the circle in half. Open it out and cut along the fold.

3.

Decorate one half circle with paint and glitter glue. Leave it to dry.

26

4.

Now cut some thread and tape it to the back of the half circle.

5.

Overlap the edges to make a cone and tape down the edge.

These make good decorations.

Make lots of cones.

Flick faces

You will need:

 large piece of paper

 paints

poster putty

round things (mugs, cups, yoghurt pots)

scrap paper

1.

Draw around the round things on scrap paper. Cut the circles out.

You can make your faces happy or sad.

Paint some specs on one of your faces.

28

2.

Stick the circles onto your paper with putty. Spread them out so that they are quite far apart.

3.

Dip a thick brush in some paint. Flick the brush from the edge of a circle outwards.

4.

Carry on flicking paint around all the circles in this way. Add lots of different colours.

5.

Peel off the paper circles and use a thin brush to paint in the faces. Leave to dry.

Fierce lion

You will need:

*large piece
of paper*

*large
plate*

paint

mug

1.

Put the plate in the middle of the paper and draw around it.

2.

Draw around the mug for eyes. Add ears, a nose and a mouth.

3.

Paint the lion's face. Add lots of spots around its nose.

4.

Paint wiggly yellow lines around the face for a mane.

5.

Add some light orange lines, then some darker orange in between.

6.

Paint a line around the lion's face. Add lots of white whiskers.

31

Frame it!

You will need:

large paper, about a hand-width bigger than your painting bright paints poster putty scrap paper stick glue small sponge

Try making other frames using different patterns.

1.

Draw round your painting on the large paper.

2.

Fold the paper in half and cut just inside the line.

3.

Stick on paper shapes with putty. Sponge on paints.

4.

Peel off the shapes and glue on the frame.

32